The Things Our Hands Once Stood For

by Martin Hayes

You are horrified at our intending to do away with private property. But in your existing society, private property is already done away with for nine-tenths of the population; its existence for the few is solely due to its non-existence in the hands of those nine-tenths.

– Karl Marx

CULTURE MATTERS

First published 2018 by **Culture Matters**, an imprint of Manifesto Press.
Culture Matters aims to promote progressive art and culture, as part of the cultural struggle for socialism. See www.culturematters.org.uk

Cover image by Paul Anthony
Other images by Martin Hayes, or commons images
Editing, layout and typesetting by Mike Quille

ISBN: 978-1-907464-32-4

Alan Dent is the founder and editor of The Penniless Press and its successor MQB. He has published five collections of poetry, a critical work on modern poetry, Too Much Toothache and many reviews. He has translated four collections of poetry from French for Smokestack Books, the latest, If The Symptoms Persist, has just been published.

Martin Hayes was born in London in 1966 and has lived in the Edgware Road/Marylebone area all of his life. He has worked in the courier industry for over 30 years, first as a leaflet distributor, then an accounts clerk, a telephonist, a courier, a controller's assistant, a controller and a control room manager. If he survives, he reckons he has 20 years left of work before retiring into a world of poverty on a state pension. He has had two collections of poems previously published, *Letting Loose The Hounds,* Redbeck Press, and, *When We Were Almost Like Men,* Smokestack Books, and he has another collection coming out in July this year called, *Roar!,* also with Smokestack.

Introduction

by Alan Dent

From Chaucer to the present day, hardly any poetry in English is about work. Most of it has been written by men from the higher reaches of society. Chaucer's father married Agnes Copton who inherited twenty-four shops, as well as other property. Chaucer himself worked for the Countess of Ulster, and one of his relatives was a moneyer.

Dunbar worked for King James, who paid him a pension estimated at about eighty pounds Scottish, a handsome amount. Edmund Spenser was educated at Merchant Taylor's, London and Pembroke, Cambridge. He served Baron Grey, owned land in the Munster Plantation and by his thirties he also owned an estate at Kilcolman.

John Donne's father died when he was four. A few months later, his mother married the wealthy Dr John Syminges. Donne was privately educated, studied at Hart Hall, Oxford, and later at Cambridge.

Keats's father was a hostler, but he rose to manage the inn where he worked. At nineteen, Keats received two bequests: one from his grandfather worth £800 and £8,000 from his mother's legacy. A total of some £550,000, at today's values.

There are exceptions, but by definition they are rare. Most of our poetry has been written by people who have not needed to work, have inherited wealth or have been paid very well. The harsh fact of employment as the means of a roof and food, and poverty or destitution being only one or two wage packets away, has been very distant from most of our poets.

By contrast, Martin Hayes writes principally about employment. Even these days it is almost a taboo topic. The legacy of the Romantics permeates contemporary poetry. The requirement to display a superior, exquisite sensibility bubbles away in the background of most poets' work. This generates what Miroslav Holub identified as a widespread failing – too much subjectivity, too much toothache.

Employment is a demeaning subject because employment is demeaning. As Hayes puts it:

we help these corporations exist
as our 83 year old mothers have to fill out 28 page forms
to see if they qualify for meals on wheels…

If part of your motivation in writing, conscious or otherwise, is to prove your superiority of response, why write from the point of view of an employee? An employee is by definition inferior. An employee is subject to an employer's contract. An employee must comply. An employee is a supplicant. An employee must please the employer, or face being demoted, thwarted or sacked. An employee must define himself or herself by promotion, remuneration, position in the hierarchy. An employee's identity is in the hands of an employer.

Like his American friend Fred Voss, Martin Hayes works for a living. He writes from the employee's perspective:

a man I work with
cries every time it gets too busy...

He works in the London courier industry, which is one of those modern, cut-throat operations ripe for zero-hours contracts and the intrusions of the so-called "gig economy". The phrase is a terrible misnomer – it ought to be called the "you-get-shafted economy".

Hayes is a husband, a father, a son, a nephew, a cousin, a friend, but none of these categories can be permitted to define our identities. Our economic system requires people to define themselves as 'hands', as employees. A good husband, wife, father, brother, son, daughter or friend is a failure if they don't have a job, status and pay. It is against this tyranny – and it is nothing less – that Hayes's poetry protests.

His style is demotic. Arguably the greatest exponent of demotic style employed for high-minded ends in English is Joe Orton, who once remarked that he came from the gutter and wasn't going to forget it. Literature isn't supposed to come from the gutter. The first working-class writer in English was Lawrence, and it is little wonder that he was snobbishly dismissed as a heretic.

Hayes, like Lawrence and Orton, is speaking for those whose lives are supposed to be not worth speaking about. Lawrence once observed that as much happens to working people as anyone else. He knew it from experience, but our culture denies it. Life happens to the rich and powerful, politicians, celebrities, magnates, pop stars with private jets, footballers with glamorous wives, and dubious businessmen with private islands. The rest become an indistinguishable mass whose experience is worthless. Only by identifying with money and power do their lives gain any significance.

Hayes is intent on revealing the significance of the lives of employees, but it isn't a pretty picture:

the controllers come in on Monday mornings
full of stories about imaginary women...

Like the employees, his poems tell stories too. Usually they are stories of the stupidity of management, impossible working conditions, unattainable deadlines or targets, exhaustion, boredom, frustration, waiting for the salary that will barely get you through the next month, depletion, breakdown, the empty boasting and fighting upwards of humiliated workers like Ronnie, who wears a t-shirt bearing the slogan:

WARNING
Madman On Duty

The photographs that accompany the poems complement them perfectly, unflinchingly conveying and criticising the realities of working life. Nearly all of the poetry books produced by the **Culture Matters** imprint show the publisher's fidelity to William Blake, the inspiration for their website, in the way they combine text with meaningful images. Here, the grainy photographs, often murky, gritty and gloomy like the world of the poems, vividly express the alienation, poverty and broken-down environment in which those 'hands' work, creating riches for others.

When he moves from the workplace to the domestic sphere, the prospect hardly improves. Browbeaten and diminished at work, men and women have little energy, confidence or relaxation to make their intimate relations rich. This is the world of Christopher Lasch's *Haven In A Heartless World*, the ironic title of his study of the way the ethos of the kill-or-be-killed workplace has invaded the private sphere, destroying the family and personal relations as an asylum from the dismal alienation of employment.

Kill-or-be-killed may seem exaggerated. People don't murder one another physically for money or advancement at work, usually – but they do murder one another emotionally and psychologically. Workplaces are snake-pits of back-biting, betrayal, sycophancy, rank-pulling, boredom tolerated in the hope of preferment, where the competition is so vicious because the stakes are so low:

it's funny really
how 37 years can seem like a couple of chicken bones in a dog's mouth
when placed alongside this technology...

says the man being dumped after nearly four decades because he can't keep up with the machines.

Disillusioned, in the best sense, this is poetry which has no need to be flowery. It is direct and simple because it is uncovering the simple truth behind our culture's manic, ceaseless, sickly, sentimental excuse-making – the human relation on which our society is based, that between employer and employee, is morally indefensible.

Out of this depressing miasma, Hayes extracts black humour. Many of his poems have a humorous edge. When employees share their experiences, they often find gallows humour, which is why employers, more and more, seek to isolate employees from one another – a distinct advantage, for them, of the you-get-shafted economy. In the humour, lies hope. That is the insight at the heart of these poems.

They rarely say it directly, but they imply, time and again, that work should belong to those who do it. Hayes applies the principle of Occam's razor – the fewer assumptions the better – and the employer's approach is full of false assumptions. Hayes is determined to expose every one, and show that those who do the work should control the work and benefit from it.

It isn't an exaggeration to say the whole of our mainstream culture, the press, television, film, music, radio, schools, the church, every bit of it, conspires to conceal this simple truth. Listen to the politicians, the commentators, the interviewers – isn't it the case that the problems they endlessly discuss emerge from the same source, the unequal relation of employer to employee?

Employment is one of the main drivers of inequality, because unequal ownership rights are built into employment relations in a capitalist economy. It is the Great Money Trick, which Robert Tressell explained in The Ragged Trousered Philanthropists, and which Karl Marx theorised as the theory of surplus value.

Along with rents from property, and interest on loans, extracting value from work done by employees is one of the means by which the few become richer than anyone should, while the majority get by and those at the bottom are doomed:

where bookies and pawnshops sit side by side
and we aren't supposed to get the irony

The means by which people are distracted from thinking about this and doing something about it are legion. Buy the latest gadget, or the new release; see the latest blockbuster, keep up with the newest fashion; download the app that will cut your toe-nails, but never stop and ask yourself why so many people hate their jobs.

It isn't work that is hateful, but employment. People like to be active. Work should be our hope. Work should be controlled by those who do it, work that is co-operative and rational, work which enchants rather than depresses. That is the vision that Hayes has glimpsed. People are bamboozled into thinking negative ideas must be shunned, but without criticism there is no ground for moral improvement. Hayes stares hard at the negative of employment and brings into the light a better possibility:

the best bits were the Friday afternoons
when the storms that poured down onto our screens all day
suddenly became a trickle..

We evolved to move horizontally, which is why our thigh muscles are so strong. We were made for walking and running long distances in search of food, better shelter, and a more propitious environment. Yet our rulers have elaborated a culture where we are pressed to move vertically. The metaphor is "the greasy pole". Perhaps a complementary one would be the escalator to nowhere.

Employment is the means to rise. We scramble for a place on the escalator, elbow and kick one another out of the way (in the most polite, Home Counties manner, of course) but if you get to the top all you find is the abyss on the other side.

Adam Smith expressed this well. He called the pursuit of private wealth a "delusion". Unfortunately, it is the delusion on which our society is based. To be deluded is to be insane or virtually insane. What Hayes writes about is the insanity of a society where employers pursue a delusion by using employees as mere conduits to their lunatic enrichment, as mere 'hands' to be employed and make money for the employer.

He is the only British poet who writes consistently and seriously about the workplace. Almost all the others ignore it. When current employment relations are consigned to the dustbin of history, and are viewed as we now view slavery, or the feudal relations between lord and vassal, will people wonder why so little was written about it? Perhaps, but maybe they'll twig that when an entire culture is in denial, ambitious writers are willing to poke out their own eyes.

Contents

BIG BUSINESS

RISE

Hands

‘these hands
are the only things that we have…’

these hands have made sandcastles too

these hands belong to a controller
and they belong to him
they get this controller into work
and they hold his cup of coffee and feed his bagel into his mouth
these hands adjust the controller's chair
that the previous controller has just left
to the required height and level
so that these hands can do their job
these hands are the only thing that this controller has these hands
have held his woman in his arms as they both together
danced and spun each other around these hands
have sent down jobs to couriers which have made their day
they have also sent down jobs to couriers
which have ruined their day these hands
have held keys to flats that are no longer theirs they have removed
a piece of glass from the screen of a child's eye these hands
have bumped and slapped other hands and held a pen to sign his name
on a marriage certificate and a divorce settlement these hands
have made sandcastles too, they have written out a bet they have
punched and gripped and the fingers that are on these hands
have helped keep this man in a job these hands
have carved out an existence for this man they have held and moulded clay
into a living thing they have made things happen these hands
move across one of their keypads like lightning
letting the fingertips attached to them
drop down on to the keypad
in a such a symphonic and synchronised way
that all of the noise stops for a minute
sometimes even for hours these hands
hold glasses of wine after sunsets and 11 hour shifts
pour them into his eager mouth they are the hands
of a controller
and even though the company that these hands work for
try continually to devise ways to detach these hands from the rest of him
they belong to all of him
and the longer he can keep on believing this
and making it happen
the more chances this controller has
of keeping hold of his job

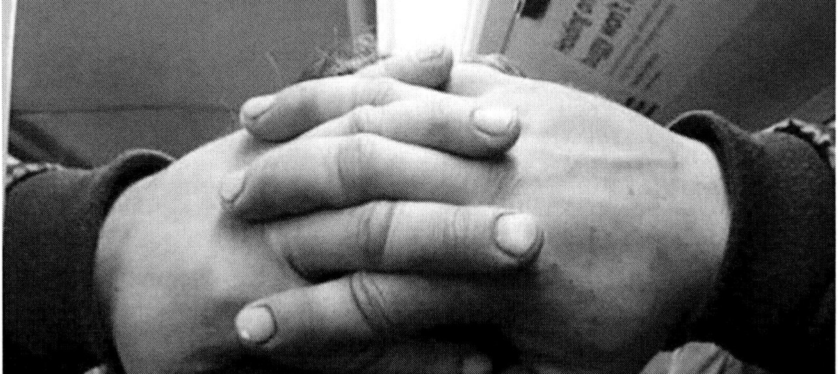

for twelve years these hands.....

for twelve years we have been making sure that this client's documents
have been picked up and arrived on time
for twelve years we have been sitting in these big comfortable controllers' chairs
prioritising this client's bookings
listening to our supervisors tell us that this client
spends enough money a month on couriers
to keep more than half of this control room
in work
for twelve years we have been making sure
that this client is looked after
because we wanted to keep hold of our jobs
and wanted to keep the couriers and other controllers
in their jobs
for twelve years we have done this
only for tonight to see on the news
that this client has been caught with its hands dipped in a pot of blood
overseeing contracts and driving deals
that eventually moved on bombs and mines
to people in countries far away
almost legally
for twelve years our hands have helped do their handiwork
picking up and delivering their menaces
not knowing that men and women and children got blown apart
because these hands,
which only ever wanted to keep hold of their jobs,
made sure that this client's contracts arrived
and got signed
on time
so that they could release the bombs
set the mines
and count the money

we help these corporations exist as our 83 year old mothers remain in pain

we help these corporations exist by making sure
that the documents of the various deals and contracts they have going on
arrive on time

we help these corporations exist
as we work through toothache
work through hangovers
pumping away at our keypads
so that the documents they send out
get there on time
and the contracts they need
can be proofread
before being sent back
to be signed

we are told by our supervisors
that these corporations spend enough money on couriers in one year
to make all of our jobs
safe

we help these corporations exist
as our 83 year old mothers have to fill out 28 page forms
to see if they qualify for meals on wheels
as our 83 year old mothers
who held down jobs for over 60 years
shit themselves on their own because the home help has been stopped
and they are too embarrassed to call a family member in to help
as our 83 year old mothers sit in homes unable to move or pick up their
grandchildren
because they have been refused an operation
to alleviate their chronic arthritis
by a government
who has received millions of pounds
from these same corporations
that we slog our guts out for each day
helping to get their documents and contracts delivered
so that they can remain healthy
and strong

our fingertips

our fingertips move like lightning across their keypads
our fingertips are the tools
of our trade they move back and forth
information that our toes and ears don't feel
our fingertips are attached to our hands
they are the fingertips they crush with chains
with pincers and hours
they are under interrogation our fingertips
are on the run they are
scratching at the earth
trying to make the tunnel big enough
so that everything else behind them can follow
our fingertips are the pickaxes of their Gulags
their owners sit in rows
tapping away at their keypads
these owners who haven't owned these fingertips
for years
for centuries
made to feel guilty that their fingertips are alive
made to feel ugly that their fingertips are unique
when they should all just be mucking in
part of their collective
with this company's heart as their heart
with this company's blood in their blood
our fingertips who have no other way to exist
other than this way of theirs
who never get to share in its profits
but who always seem to get to share
in its losses

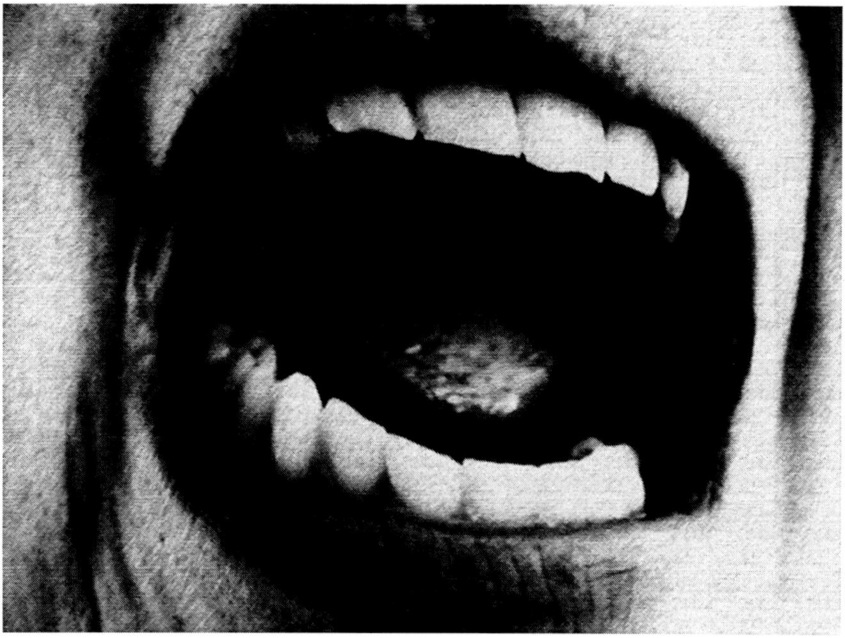

dealing with the anger

the men who own hands
that'll never pull a pair of silk socks over their feet
the men who own throats
that'll never feel the contents of a £100 bottle of wine
slip down them
the men who own mouths
full of teeth that keep them awake at night
knowing that they'll never be able to afford
to get them filled
or capped
the men who own habits
who come in every morning
twitching like something caught in a trap
only to turn into swollen superstars
after their mid-morning snort

the men who own council tenancies
with years of service stored inside their hearts
who live in constant fear
of the new automated allocating system
taking away their jobs and their homes
the men who own memories
of what it was like to be young and fearless
with only iron in your heart and fire in your guts
who now
whenever a supervisor comes out
to bollock them for fucking up a job
lower their heads
and dig their nails into the palms of their hands
because that was the best way they knew
the only way they knew
how to stop the guts that they still had left
from making them do something
that might place all of what they believed in and loved
at risk

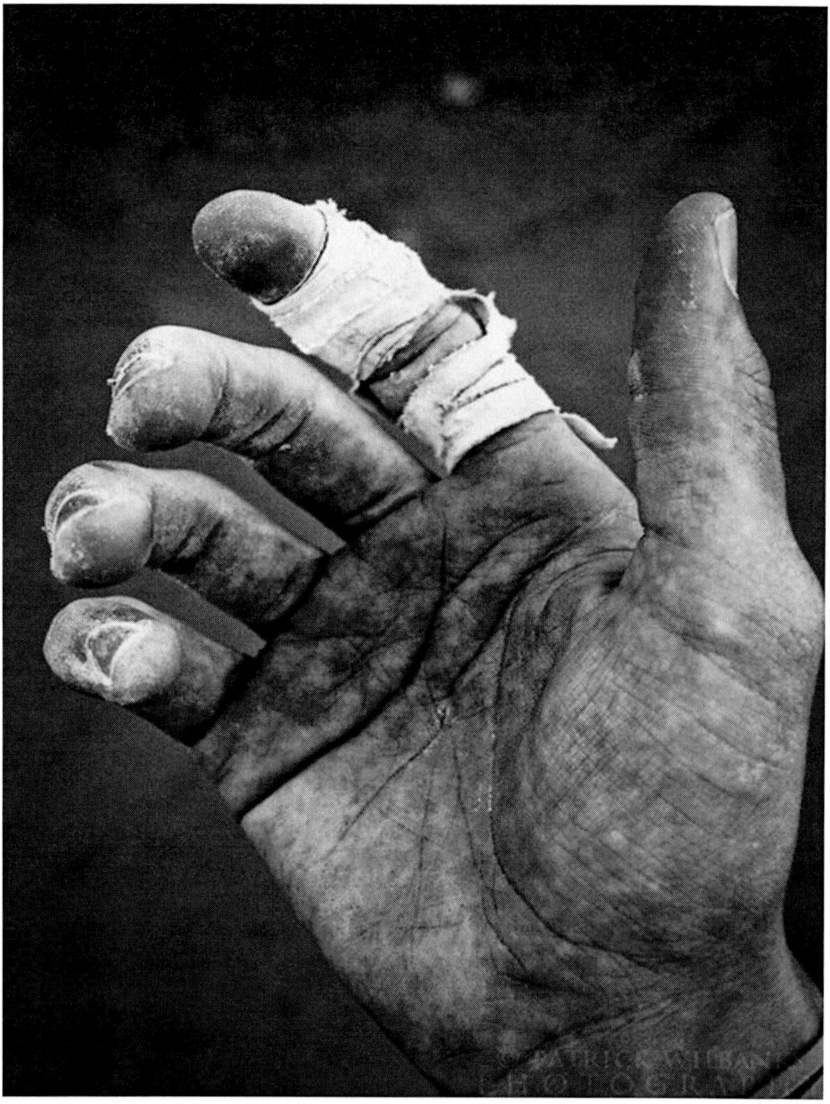

the things our hands once stood for

the new automated allocating system will not need
hands
to press buttons to send down jobs to couriers
the new automated allocating system will do that automatically
it will not need a man to cover it while it takes a lunch break
a man to sit in its seat while it takes its 20 days paid holiday a year
a man to look after its couriers whenever it calls in sick
because the new automated allocating system won't ever take lunch breaks
it won't ever need holidays
and it will never ever call in sick
the new automated allocating system won't need the men who for years
have sat in front of their screens working out which couriers should get which jobs
the men whose hands have helped build this company the same
hands
that once helped rivet together the Humber bridge
weld pipes together 2000 feet under the North Sea
that ran gas into villages and cities
that placed a cherry on top of a cake in a baker's on a high street long ago shut
replaced by Subway McDonalds Starbucks Express chains Pound shops
where bookies and pawn shops sit side by side
and we aren't supposed to get the irony
hands
that drop change into the homeless woman's polystyrene cup
because they know that it could be them next
hands
that came from hands who once picked up a shovel to dig a trench
on a battlefield of a war they didn't start
from hands that pickaxed at rock 200 feet under Newcastle
freeing the coal that would power
this progress that these hands are now not a part of
progress that has seen jobs disappear or moved overseas leaving hands behind
that still need to open a tin of beans throw a steak onto a griddle pan
break open an egg
hold a pint of milk stick a fork into sausages
feed them into his mouth
hands
that pay rent electricity bills dentist bills council tax insurance premiums
hold their women
at night under skies that break open in thunder that once hung doors

in council flats schools and libraries
welded ships together
replaced the heart or kidney of an 8 year old boy
hands
that soon won't even be needed anymore
whose only use will be
to pick up a pen and write a poem
about the things our hands
once stood for

Controllers

'with smiles,
that have no right to exist...'

the men I work with

a man I work with
cries every time it gets too busy
throws his head back onto his fat neck
and stares up into the ceiling
all the while muttering under his breath
how thankful he is that he still has a job
and hasn't been allowed to die yet

a man I work with
goes home every night to make Airfix models
only to hang them from his ceiling
or spread them out across his attic floor
reenacting the battle of Midway
or the siege of Leningrad
talking all day about historical wonders
and what men and women have been capable of before

a man I work with
goes to the toilet every hour
to snort himself out
and comes back
like a Viking halfway through raping himself through a village
only to administer a masterclass in controlling
that text books could be written about

a man I work with
gets so drunk in the nights after his shifts have finished
that when he comes in for work the next morning
he looks as small as a little death rattle
rattling away at his keypad
with eyes that shine through his pain
and a smile on his face
that has no right to exist

the men I work with
haven't written any great books
that everyone talks about
they haven't painted any great pictures
or composed a symphony
that can bring a tear to the eye

but they have worked for years doing 11 hour shifts in a dead-end job
they have spent years getting screamed and shouted at by supervisors
so that those supervisors could feel like they were 8 feet tall

they have spent years tapping away at keypads
sending instructions to couriers to drive their big vans to recently shutdown offices
to remove desks and chairs still warm from the redundant arses
that used to sit on them earning just enough money to pay their rent years
spent tapping away at those buttons
sending instructions to couriers to whizz through the streets
so they can collect the blood of a £500 an hour private healthcare patient
and deliver it to a lab so that the results can be returned within 45 minutes
as 83 year old women die in corridors waiting for an extra blanket years
tapping away at those buttons
sending instructions for men to go and pick up the forgotten hat of a pop star
the forgotten shawl of a millionaire actress the forgotten
shoes of a £1,000 an hour model the forgotten bow tie of a CEO
only to drive like lunatics through the streets risking their lives
just so they can get them back into their soft hands years
spent making sure that the documents and contracts of the Great companies arrive
before the deadline
so that padlocks can be snapped shut on the doors of a factory for the last time
and playgrounds in which they grew up in
in which they drank their first can of beer in smoked their first cigarette in played
kiss chase in
can be turned into building sites where cranes will raise yet another block of luxury
flats
up out of the Earth

these men I work with
who haven't written any great books painted any great pictures
composed any symphonies
but who
just by the act of living and carrying on
being controllers
help keep the world up in the sky
the birds on wires singing the soil moist in a pair of hands the
flowers and stars burning bright with meaning with those smiles
that have no right to exist
a million times more genuine and stirring
than any of those great pieces of art
could ever be

a controller's image is everything

the controllers come in on Monday mornings
full of stories about imaginary women
that they fucked over the weekend,
they drag themselves through the control room
like men who've just walked out of a desert
pretending to be exhausted
and close to death
chucking themselves down into their chairs
waiting for somebody to ask them, "what's the matter?"
wincing any time somebody came to close to them
telling them to be careful,
"because she must've been a tiger or something
the way she's opened up my back,"
taking every opportunity
to let their colleagues know
how their tongues feel like the seized-up calf muscle
of a marathon runner,
how their bollocks have never felt so drained,
their cocks so sore,
drinking can after can of Red Bull,
not giving up the charade
until they think everybody
has got the message

obviously
spending your entire weekend
sitting in front of the telly
getting drunk on cider and wine,
reading all of the tabloids and the Racing Post,
doing Channel 4's
Super-Six,
watching X Factor, porn videos
and Ant and Dec,
every now and then sending out
for curry or Chinese,
waiting to see if your lottery numbers come up
without one ring on the phone
and no one to call
is not the sort of image
our controllers feel comfortable with

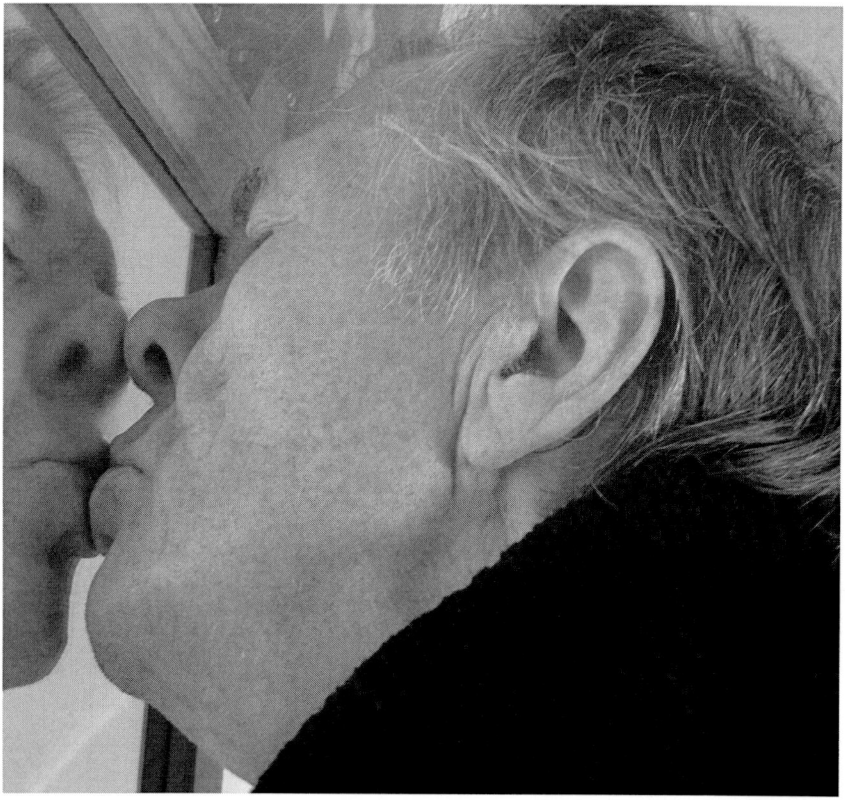

the bodies of kings

the two bodybuilder mechanics and three bodybuilder controllers
used to bodybuild together at the gym every lunch time and after work
and there was a fierce rivalry between all of them
as they compared bicep circumferences and thigh-muscle circumferences
always with a neon or shit-coloured protein drink in their hands
walking around the control room screwing up their faces in utter disgust
at what their colleagues fed into their mouths
walking around the workshop in t-shirts two sizes too small for them
their biceps and shoulders stretching that material
flexing their muscles every now and then like glistening stallions
under a Kentucky sun
as they spoke in almost revered tones about bench presses and squats and 120 k-g
as though they were their gods
looking out of those ever decreasing pupils of theirs
and down along their noses at the drunk controllers
who couldn't get through a night without a drink
coming in looking tired and beaten
wishing the day away
just so they could get at another drink;
at the fat and obese telephonists
who couldn't get through a day without their fix of burger and chips
continually munching away in between on Doritos and cheese balls
and Haribos and chocolate;
at the couriers who had no time for anything else
other than keeping down the 3 jobs they juggled
who only ever wanted to talk about the different ways they could sell their labour
so that their hands could earn as much money as possible
before they died;
as the body builders strolled home like panthers
only to sit naked on their beds
with their legs apart up in the air
waxing themselves ripping off every last hair
from their arse-cracks and perineums and scrotums
administering enemas to themselves just before they go to bed
trying to drain every last drop of fluid
out of those bodies of kings

not everyone can be as focused and disciplined
as those bodybuilders though

some of us have fucking lives to live

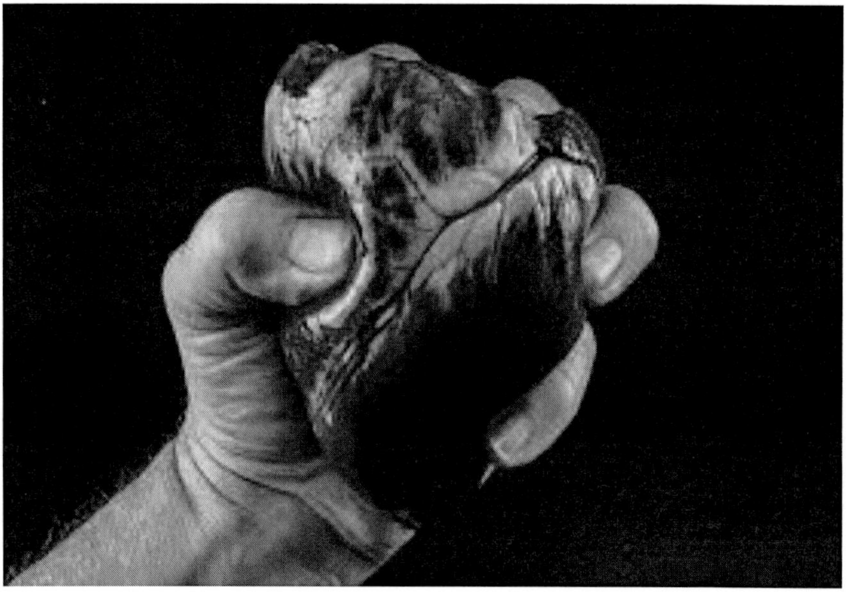

a new hot 38-year-old girlfriend

Dermot gets sent pictures and texts on his phone
from his new hot 38 year old girlfriend
revealing to him her breasts
or detailing what she plans to do to him
when he gets home from his 11 hour shift

Dermot goes around the control room
showing these pictures and texts from his new hot 38 year old girlfriend
to his fellow controllers
hoping they will understand how lucky he is
and why he is now tired and exhausted
due to her demands on him
in the bedroom
and the hallway
and the kitchen
rather than before
when he was always tired and exhausted
from dealing with all of the abusive texts
and the pictures of bills
that had just dropped through the letterbox
that his ex-wife used to send him

Dermot is still as skint as before
and he still owes the same companies
the thousands of pounds that he owed them before
but it is important for him to let his fellow controllers know
that he is tired and exhausted now
in a different way,
for a different reason,
a way that makes him want to smile and share things,
a way that makes him feel proud
to be a man
amongst all these other
debt-laden men

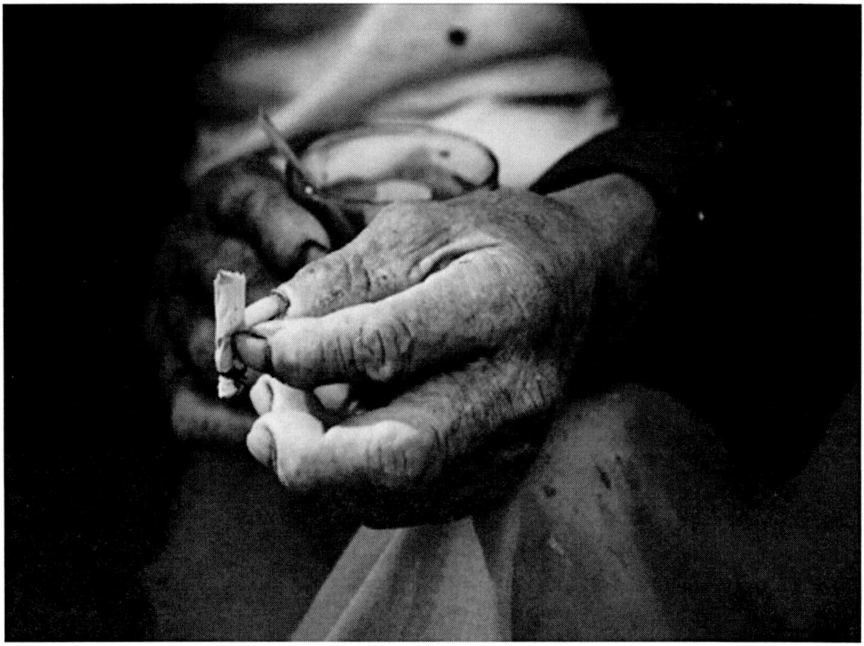

Ronnie's new t-shirt

the new guy leant over and asked me
why Ronnie keeps on mumbling to himself?
"you'll find out come Friday afternoon," I said,
but we didn't have to wait till then
we didn't have to wait until it got too busy
for Ronnie to handle once again
causing him to throw that head of his
back onto the rolls of fat that were his neck
staring up at the ceiling
all the while squeezing away at that big stress-ball of his
so that it disappeared
inside one of his big wrestler palms,
all the while with his eyes wide open
drilling up through that ceiling looking up, up
and away into the stars
repeating over and over
almost in a whisper
that mantra of his
which none of us could quite ever catch
which none of us ever dared ask him about

no
we didn't have to wait till then
before the new guy found out why Ronnie seemed so odd
and put everyone around him
on high alert
because two minutes after he asked me
Ronnie stood up to take his jean-jacket off
only to reveal a new t-shirt of his
which had the words

WARNING!
Madman On Duty!

printed on its front

when you join Phoenix Express
sometimes
the realisation that you are working in an actual lunatic asylum
can come sooner than expected

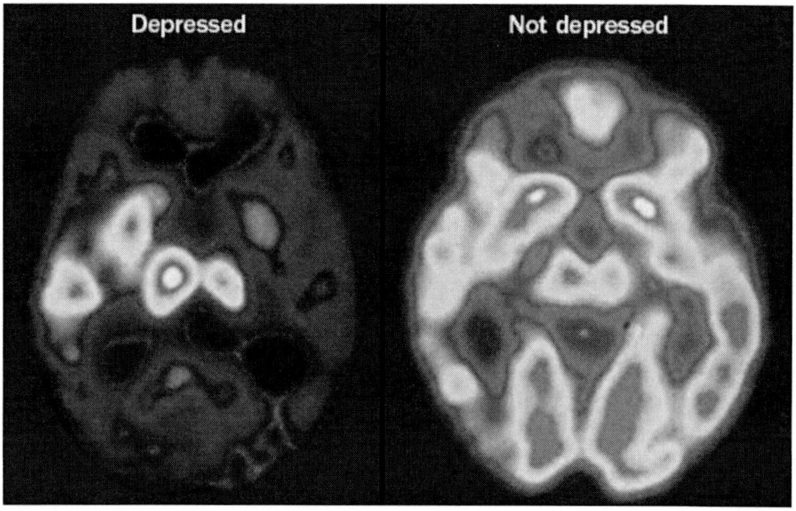
Depressed
Not depressed

supervisors in fear of Ronnie

the supervisors care about Ronnie
they worry about his mental health
they put him on report
so that they can keep a closer eye on him
their sick little child
their sick little chameleon

the supervisors care about Ronnie
they are concerned that he doesn't always remember
the rules
that he might one day set fire to their office
might put MDMA in their coffee once again
or else climb onto the roof
and refuse to come down

the supervisors care about Ronnie
they call him in for counselling sessions
to discuss how he is getting on
hollowing out his tunnel
plucking the barbed wire from his eyes
finding other crew members
to come with him on his trip to the sun

the supervisors care more than Ronnie's mother cared
more than Ronnie's father cared
more than Ronnie's social worker cared
they care so much
that they have told Ronnie
that soon he might not be able to use their facilities
to play anymore
in case he injures himself
or worse
injures one of them

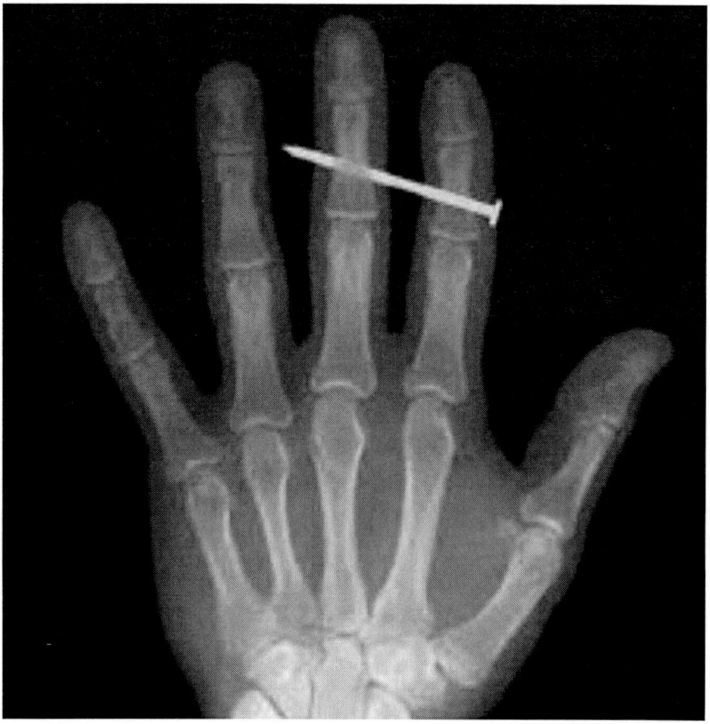

banned from shooting up nails into a tin ceiling like a cowboy

Ronnie has been banned from going down to the workshop in his lunch hour
he has been banned from going in there
and picking up the workshop's nail gun and waving it around in the air
shooting nails up into the tin ceiling like a cowboy
banned from picking up those big wide-mouthed spanners in his hands
and chucking them at the walls like a circus knife thrower
banned from laying out 10 tyres side by side on the floor and running through them
stamping his feet through the center of each one
like a marine in training
banned from picking up exhaust systems
and holding them in one hand behind his shoulder
pretending to launch them into the air like an Olympic javelin thrower
banned from removing the sump plugs on engines
so that the oil inside them pours out onto the floor
while running around screaming at the top of his voice,
"MAYDAY! MAYDAY!
GET ALL OF THE BIRDS TO SAFETY!
I THINK WE HAVE AN OIL SLICK ON OUR HANDS!"
banned
from taking the air-hose and placing it in his mouth
before pulling back the silver trigger
that made all of his hair stand up and his eyes to bulge
banned from grabbing 3 or 4 of those mega-sized towel rolls
and going up to the mezzanine floor
before launching them off into the air
so that they streamed out and down onto the workshop floor
all the while screaming "ARGEN-TINA! ARGEN-TINA!"
banned
from sitting down with the mechanics while they tried to eat their lunch
and telling them that all of these tools and stuff
that they have to play with makes him feel horny

which was okay
and understandable
but no help to us controllers
who are now going to have to work out a way
to contain all of those fantasies
that run about inside Ronnie's head
while we eat
our lunch

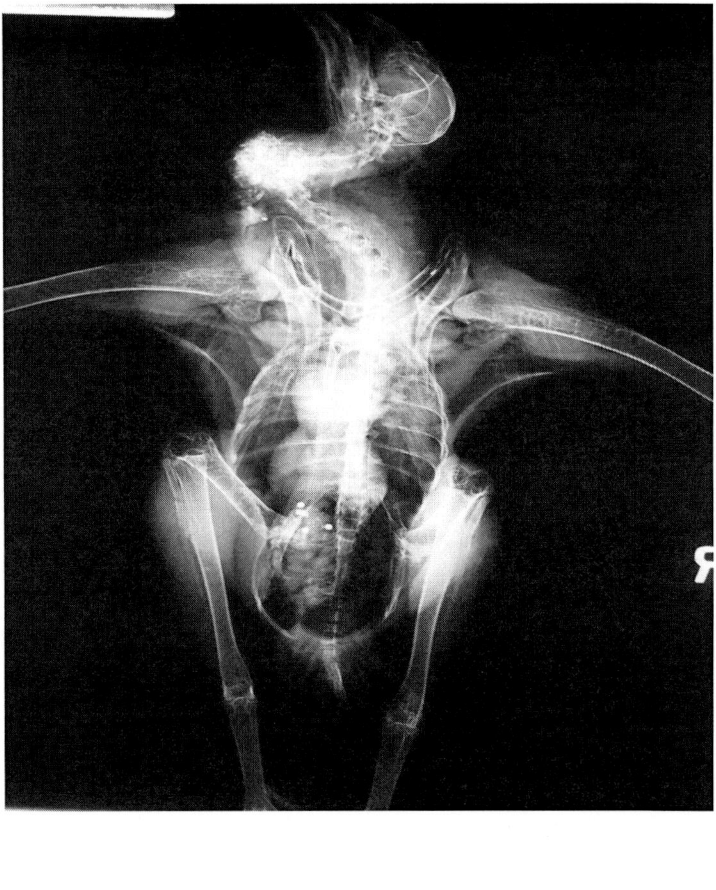

Ronnie and the swans

now that Ronnie has been banned from going down to the workshop and playing with all of their tools
he has started going over to Sainsbury's to buy a loaf of bread
and then taking that loaf of bread down to the canal
spending his whole lunch break sitting on one of the benches on the footpath by the side of the canal
tearing off bits of that bread
and feeding it to the swans
and as they all paddle towards the spot Ronnie sits at
Ronnie has started talking to them
asking them questions about life and the Universe
convincing those swans that he means them no harm by smiling and oohing and ahhing at them
dropping the torn off bits of bread a little bit closer to him each time
until finally they had to haul their swan arses out of that canal
and come closer and closer to Ronnie if they wanted to get at that bread
as Ronnie kept reeling them in
naming them
talking to them in the sweetest voice he could manage,
"hello, Snowy, you're looking fine today,
I hope nobody ever kills you
and breaks that lovely neck of yours,"
and, "hey,
Flip-Flop,
come to Daddy,
you know Daddy loves you,"
until after a month or so
he had those swans eating bread out of the palm of his hand

4 or 5 swans padding away around Ronnie's feet
as he tore off that bread and fed it to his new babies
with a heart warm enough that it heated up his whole being
"everything, for once, is going to be alright,"
Ronnie kept muttering to himself

as the clouds began gathering above his head
and Winter got ready
to make everything dead again

Workers

'some men
are just far more capable
of doing almost anything
than other men
I guess…'

lifting off like eagles into the sky

the best bits were the Friday afternoons
when the storms that poured down onto our screens all day
suddenly became a trickle
when all the men in there suddenly became excited
as the night and weekend shone at us from the end of that little bit of tunnel left

Marlon getting up from his controller's chair every fifteen minutes
announcing to everyone, "there is a lucky lady out there right now fellas,
and she doesn't even know it yet," as he clapped his hands together and let out a roar

as Stevie sat back with a big Cheshire-cat grin on his face
rubbing his hands together in anticipation so fast that smoke rose up from the palms of his hands

as Norm ran up and down the control room aisle faster than usual
as he played up to his colleagues' laughter
doing that "ooh-aah, lad" pirate impression of his

as Marcus made paper aeroplanes out of the memos we'd received that day
that Antoine his right-hand man plucked out of that air and crushed into paper balls
before throwing them back up
letting them fall until they were the exact height for him to smack them sideways with his hip
before spinning around 1 2 3 times on the spot
all the while firing off imaginary bullets from the fingers he'd shaped into guns on his chest

as Tony spoke in almost revered tones
about the amount of rosé and beer he was going to drink
before passing out and forgetting everything
as Dermot stood in the middle of the room
stretching and flexing those muscles of his telling anyone who would listen
that he was limbering up
because he had it on good authority
that he was going to be involved in a 48 hour bout of Turkish wrestling
with his new hot 38 year old girlfriend

and then there was Ronnie
who would just sit there
with his arms folded and a look on his face
that didn't understand what was going on why
these men he worked with all week who seemed that whole week
to be stuck in that same pit of depression he was always in
were now suddenly lifting off like eagles into the sky
were now talking about this great life they all had
as though the women and beer and wine they were about to ingest
was going to equalise all of that pain
make it all ok
when in reality
they'd all just be back in on Monday
feeling it again

some men
will just never understand or get
what a Friday afternoon means
to other men

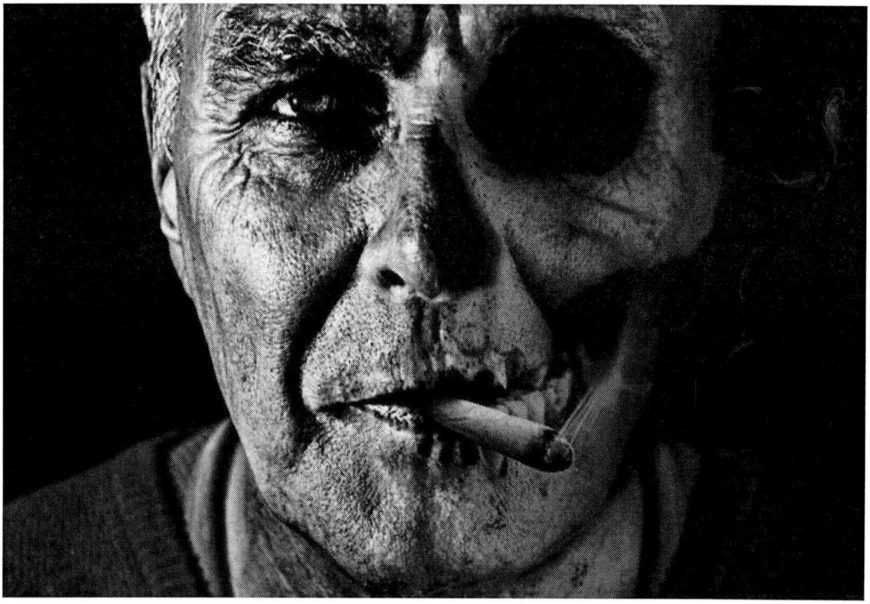

the sun didn't rise today

Timmy was special
he used to call on for work at 7 am every morning
smack right in the centre of London
ready for anything his controller gave him
and when the jobs started coming in
he'd accept them on his PDA as quick as a flash
easing that van of his into gear, eating up the road
and by 9 o'clock
when most of the other couriers were just waking up
or else calling in for work from home
he'd already have 6 jobs under his belt

then as things started hotting up
Timmy would move into another gear
flinging that van of his around the streets
accepting everything his controller sent him
never having to use an A-to-Z or sat nav
with all of the pick-up addresses and delivery addresses he had on his schedule
beeping away inside his head
like a holographic map
as they all moved like on a gyroscope
every time he turned that steering wheel of his
his whole mind the same as a screen
in front of a NASA control mission centre

as he suddenly turned off main roads
to scoot off down alleyways just about wide enough to take his van
snaking off through back-doubles
that not even black cab drivers knew about
only to reappear 400 yards back up on the main road
ahead of the traffic
and whenever he got to a collection or delivery address
he'd park that van of his half-on half-off of pavements
leaping out of his van in a blur
so fast he hadn't ever got a ticket in over 6 years
constantly drinking coffee from that big metal flask of his
constantly plucking sugar-coated cola-bottles from that big bag
he kept between his thighs
flicking them up into his mouth
jabbering away on his radio

screaming at his controller, "give me more! give me more!"
all day for 11 hours straight
without a break or anything to eat
never slowing down
relentless as a Spartan
until finally he would turn that van of his towards home
having accumulated the work of 3 men
bibbing his horn
as he headed up Tottenham Court Rd towards Camden
with over 30 jobs and £150
in his pocket

until that Monday
when he didn't call on at 7 am like he always did
everyone in the control room commenting on it
like it was the same as the sun not coming up today
all of us
finding out later that he had topped himself
sat on the balcony of his flat
where he must've decided that whatever it was
he couldn't take it anymore
and opened that vein
that usually held in all of that extra-special blood of his
blood that made him better than 3 men

Ronnie
commenting later that,
"some men
are just far more capable
of doing almost anything
than other men
I guess."

beano

the mechanics outdid even themselves
on their latest beano down to Southend
with Scott not even making it there
detained at Loughton services
for pissing in a rubber plant next to the Cashino one armed bandits
and then Craig
falling off the pier as soon as he got there
standing up on the railings as he acted out the scene from Titanic
before a gust of wind lifted him up and over the side and Paul
passing out on a bench overlooking the sea
having drunk too much out of Smithy's flask of mushroom tea
and then after midday
Ben getting into a fight on the promenade
with the chicken mascot for Chicken Cottage
ripping his headpiece off and chucking it up into the wind
so that it careered off and landed in the lap of a child's buggy
and Smithy playing the £1-a-go bingo slots
only to disappear with a woman old enough
to be his grandmother
and Liam
breaking his ankle as he tried to jump from his dodgem
into Chris's dodgem
only to fall short and get run over
by a dodgem driven by two old age pensioners

the thousands of hours spent in Phoenix Express's workshop
changing clutches and oil filters
having to lift whole engines out of vans on wrenches and pulleys using
all of their strength to lower those engines down
onto their workbench like a feather,
the thousands of hours spent in the Siberian cold of that workshop
laying on that floor that seeped all of its cold into the bones of their backs
as they peered up into exhaust systems and suspension systems
trying to service vehicles so they could make those 130,000-mile vans and bikes
start up like brand new machines
had obviously taken its toll on our mechanics

nothing though
that a day out at the seaside
couldn't put right

peace

the mechanics sought peace while stuck under those 130,000-mile
vans
trying to clean and replace oil filters and carburettors
so that those vans could be rolled out of their workshop
as good as new
the mechanics sought peace while staring into the bikes that had been brought into
their workshop
dying
staring into their engines while their burnt and red fingers twisted back the revs
resting their ears as close to those engines as they could possibly get
just so they could hear and feel the illnesses of those bikes
inside their guts
as their fingers twisted away and turned at the caps on those engines
trying to heal them
the mechanics
who lived in rooms within rented flats filled with men who also sought peace
sharing their lives with men who washed cars
and moved the contents of offices into other offices for less than the cost of a
burrito
per hour
men who propped themselves up on their pillows at night seeking peace
by drinking cans of cheap beer and eating kebabs
skyping their families far away in other
countries
men who got up at 5 am every morning feeling rejuvenated
to march at the sun and swallow the universe
putting up scaffolding or delivering boxes
for men who weren't anywhere near
the men that they were

the mechanics sought peace under those 130,000-mile vans
because they didn't have a fig tree to sit under like Buddha did
the mechanics who tried to heal those dying bikes with their fingers and hearts
because they didn't have a woman to hold at night
the mechanics who couldn't afford anything more
other than to exist in their rooms within rented flats
filled with other men all seeking the same type of peace that eagles gliding
through the immense sky feel

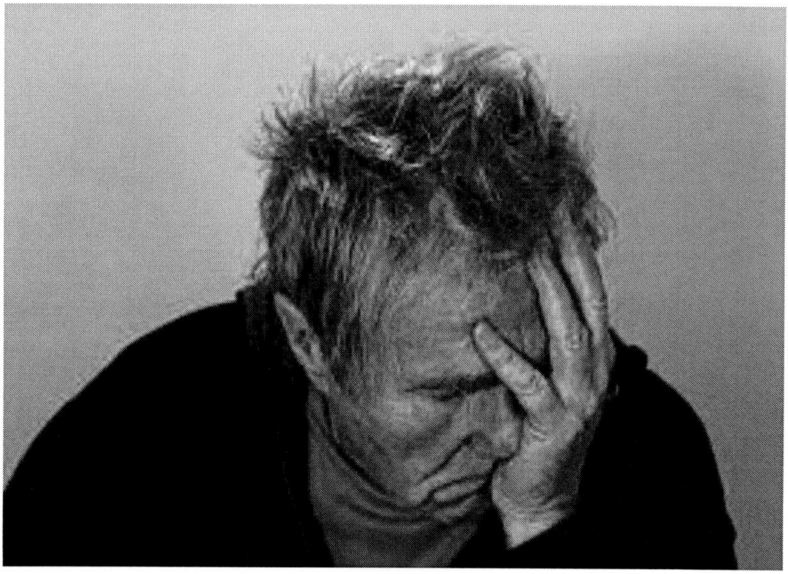

a couple of chicken bones in a dog's mouth

if you listened to Ray
the 37 years he's spent in control rooms
has been his saviour

"the only thing that kept me feet on the ground, son,
the only thing that kept me feet on the ground"

the first thing he did every morning
was take the anti-static wipes
and clean down his keypad and monitor
making sure that there was a pen and paper by his side
some coffee a working phone
and a jug of tap water

he delighted in telling the less experienced controllers
stories about the past
"you had to control with your wits back then, lad,
there wasn't any of this computer bullshit,
when couriers got pissed off
they used to come up the office for a straightener,
none of this 'fill out a complaint form please
and we'll get back to you' stuff,
they were there, right in your face,
and you had to just deal with it,
got these scars that way, lad"

the 37 years Ray had spent in a control room
must've had something to do with the two weeks' notice he got
when it became obvious,
when it just couldn't be hidden anymore
that he was never,
not even in another 37 years,
going to grasp the new high-tech operating system
that had recently been installed

and as Ray said
after he told us the news,
"it's funny really,
how 37 years can seem like a couple of chicken bones in a dog's mouth
when placed alongside this technology"

Progress

'...to sit around tables bigger than the sun
squeezing away at peoples lives
like they were plastic cups...'

trying to paint the Sistine Chapel over again

the four programmers brought in to develop the new automated allocating system
have spent the last 18 months shut away in their office writing code
trying to replicate the knowledge of us controllers
in digital format
but for the last 6 weeks
those same developers
have strangely abandoned their office
and come out to sit with us controllers
asking us questions about why we make this decision
and that decision
all the while writing down notes in their little Moleskine books
that will apparently help
hone their monster

we conduct show-and-tell lessons with them
highlighting that our decisions are not always the same
given the same circumstances
because you have to know the abilities of the couriers that are available
as well as the client's expectations
and that that was what us controllers called
a moving target
which we had to hit more often than not
or else lose our jobs

obviously they hadn't listened or quite understood
how complex this controlling lark really is
because if they had
then they wouldn't have signed off on a new automated allocating system
that goes live next week
which won't be able to paint the Sistine Chapel over again
which won't be able to leap like a Nureyev
which won't be able to carve marble like a Rodin
and which won't be able to see the unseen
or think the unthinkable
quite like us controllers can

but then that isn't the point of the new automated allocating system
the point is to try and force it through
so that directors can sit around tables bigger than the sun
squeezing away at people's lives like they were plastic cups
only to finally be able to reveal to their shareholders
that they might just have found
a new way of doing it
a new way to fly straight through the centre of that sun
while reducing the wage bill of controllers
by at least 10 times 30 grand a year
for ever

threatened again

the week before the new automated allocating system was to be introduced
the HR manager called all of us controllers in
one by one
to assure us that our jobs were safe
and to tell us that we needed to embrace this new technology
and see it as a tool
that will help us to do our jobs even more efficiently
than we were currently doing

unfortunately
they hadn't told the supervisors this
who spent the whole week picking us up on minor issues
before delighting in telling us not to worry
because next week,
after the new automated allocating system has been introduced,
we most probably won't have a job
anyway

the new automated allocating system

of course it made us all feel uneasy
of course it made us all feel paranoid
and worry if we were going to keep these jobs
that paid our rent and bills and fed our families

of course the rumours that its tentacles
armed with a billion sensors
could reach out into everywhere
and suck up all of the information inside our theatre
turning it into little bits
that it could put back together again more beautifully
than any of us controllers could
made us feel threatened

of course the rumours that its artificial brain
which didn't take lunch breaks
or get paid 20 days holiday a year
which didn't drink alcohol or fall sick
or need a woman to hold it in its arms
which didn't have to worry about paying the rent
or the mobile phone contracts
or feed the electricity key
which never forgot a thing
and had the streets and one-way systems of London
and all of the clients' service level agreements
programmed into its metallic cortex
made us feel nervous and inadequate

of course all of that propaganda and rumour
made us controllers confide in each other
and to share with each other
that this must be how those Londoners must've felt
back in the Blitz

the new automated allocating system
had made the controllers
for the very first time ever
seek ways to hold hands
and think about how best we could all
stick together

finally in harmony together

Dermot placed his arm around Tony's shoulder
on the walk up the road to catch the bus home
after their shifts had finished

Marcus started speaking
to his fellow controllers across the lunch table
rather than sitting there all aloof and superior

Stevie gave up putting a palmful of salt
into his fellow controllers' coffee
whenever they weren't looking

Mikey offered to cover the hour Bart needed off
to go and collect his sick mother
from the hospital

and when Controller Donnelly went to buy a drink
he also brought one back for Antoine
his right-hand man

even Ronnie had put down that stress-ball of his
and that mad stare of his
and started trying to engage with his fellow controllers
pretending as best he could
that he didn't feel like an outsider
who was slowly going mad

this new automated allocating system
that was set to go live next week
was having a strange effect
on these men who normally wouldn't cross the road
to piss on each other
even if they were on fire

anger and agony

the programmers of the new automated allocating system
have finally admitted that it doesn't work
and have advised the board of directors
to withdraw its use
so that they can spend more time tinkering with the logic
that the new automated allocating system uses
to allocate out the jobs

that's more time
getting paid their 70 grand a year salaries
trying to come up with an algorithm
that us controllers already have
seared inside our heads

that's more time
trying to understand the various circumstances
us controllers understand
as easily as we pull on our socks
which we are able to compute
so that we make correct decisions
98 times out of 100
but which the new automated allocating system fluffs
more often than not
sending couriers down jobs they shouldn't get

that's more time
working from home drinking Red Bulls and smoothies
taking breaks to mow the lawn
or skype their programming mates
to discuss other projects
they have going on
as us controllers have to sit in our controllers' chairs for 11 hours a day
on less than half their money
continuing to make decisions
that keeps this 22 million pounds a year company going
talking to couriers and customers about their problems
and instantly solving them
with no time left to pay our rent or our gas bill
with no time left to challenge the county court judgments
or our overdrawn bank charges

with no time left
to consider that if we didn't keep on doing this
then we might even be able to paint a picture
or write a novel
or carve from a piece of steel
a perfect image to represent
our anger and agony

the programmers return

after 4 months away in the Dordogne
the programmers of the new automated allocating system
have returned.

they look healthy and strong
as they announce that they think they are almost there
transferring the knowledge and guile of us controllers
into their metallic bastard.

their little metallic bastard
who once grown up and able to think properly
will take away all of our jobs,
which if all goes according to plan
will leave this control room completely empty of men,
completely empty except for the purring and whirring
of its gigantic brain
stuffed away inside a little black box
sat on a table in the middle of this room
on a black piece of felt
like a mysterious piece of alien art
which no one is allowed to see
which no one is allowed to understand
and no laughter
anywhere.

Housing

'just one ugly block of council flats still stands
sat there like a rotten tooth
in a row of perfect mollars…'

the bed and breakfast place

the bed and breakfast place
that took up all of the floors above the three shops and pub
three streets down from the office
has shut down

the bed and breakfast place where some of the couriers
down on their luck or in between homes
used to take out one-week rents
so that they had somewhere to come back to after their 11 hour shifts
to dry their leathers and undershirts on the Victorian radiators
that creaked and hissed all night
where they were able to drink themselves warm again
or heat up soup on gas rings before
laying down in a bed with one hand still gripped to the ladder
has shut down
because the landlord has decided
that it'd be better to sell the 33 years left on the lease
to property developers

it will not be long
before the three shop owners and owner of the pub decide to do the same
and the developers can then knock it all down
and build another glass and marble block of luxury flats
and then the couriers and mechanics
and other men and women
who relied on that bed and breakfast place
while down on their luck or in between homes
will have had their grip on the ladder prised open
a little bit more,
some of them completely,
but nobody will see them falling,
nobody will see them disappearing below the surface
or worry what they will do
to stop themselves from drowning

all that will happen
is people will comment on how the area
is changing for the better
and turn their eyes away
as they disappear
under the water

debt
Microsoft

the employed poor

they have a car a job with no contract they work for a company that has
a zero-tolerance policy on sick days and non-attendance they have a
flat with heating and food they have a bottle of wine of a night
they cook a pasta dinner for their two kids they try to buy their
kids' new clothes and a mobile phone but it's never the right
ones always 2 or 3 generations behind they are healthy but
nervous strong but fragile they have nothing in their
hands or tucked away under their beds they
are only one withheld monthly pay cheque
away from disaster one boss's decision
away from hunger one unfortunate
accident away from annihilation
one unplanned bill away from
tipping point one illness
away from seeing the
whole edifice of
their lives come
tumbling down
with no one
around to
help put
any of it
back
together
again

MALLARD

one block of council flats left

just one block of council flats remains in this area
where we work our magic
allocating out jobs to couriers
so that multinationals and £500 an hour law firms
and hedge fund managers who look after billions of pounds
can remain healthy and strong
making more money in one hour
than all the tenants of this last block of council flats left
will make in their lifetimes
put together

just one ugly block of brick and red cladding council flats still stands
amongst all of the million-pound lofts and chrome and smoked-glass luxury flats
that have sprung up in this area over the last 8 years just one
block with 42 flats
where couriers and mechanics and schoolteachers and bus drivers
and nurses and firemen and waitresses can still safely keep
a roof over their families' heads where they can
still wash and cook and put their children into a bed
and get them up to go into a school this one block of flats left
sat there like a rotten tooth in a row of perfect molars
housing these workers
enabling them to keep their dignity and love as millionaire footballers
move in next door as seven-figure-waged bankers buy whole floors
just so they can have somewhere to stay while in London
as people in the media hire cranes
to lift £30,000 pieces of furniture into their lofts as
politicians and councillors plot
how best they can make this last ugly block of council flats
disappear
along with its infections

how many shifts must a controller put in before he picks up a saxophone or pen

how many shifts must a controller put in before he realises
that this country he calls his own has disowned him
and couldn't care less if he starved or even if he didn't have a roof
to cover his head

how many hours does a controller have to put up with
getting screamed and shouted at by supervisors paid 4 times more
just because he wasn't able to get the forgotten passport of a CEO
delivered back into his hands before his flight took off
so he could board that flight
and fly halfway around the globe to sign a contract that will level a forest flood a plain cause
whole communities to have to move on
before
that controller realises
that the migrants he blames for taking all of the flats
for draining the treasury of his tax pounds in undeserved benefits
are not the problem
but that the government he voted in who he sings songs for
whose national flag he has had tattooed on his calf
are

how many hours of toil and pressure must the controller endure before he accepts
the reason why his pay cheque still says the same as it did
in 2012
is not because of the migrant workers flooding our streets living under
every manhole cover eating
everything green hanging from the trees raping
and grooming their daughters that
the real reason why
are the policies of this country he beats his chest for buys team-shirts of stands
in pubs rowing with mates about who had the greatest empire ever on earth

how many youth clubs libraries and post offices need to be knocked down
to be replaced by blocks of luxury flats
before that controller stops blaming those same immigrants
for taking all of the flats and all of the NHS beds for him to realise

that he's been part of a magic trick a hypnosis that has just convinced him
they are

how many cranes
need to stand guard in the sky
waiting to lift block of marble after block of marble glistening handrail after
glistening handrail
air-conditioning ventilation water sprinkler jacuzzi steam room and shower systems
up to the top floors of those luxury flats before that controller
lays down his anger and stops blaming the Somalian Brazilian Colombian Nigerian
East European black
man and black woman Muslim and Jew
and picks up a saxophone or a pen
to announce to the world that he has finally understood
and wants to link arms with all of his sisters and brothers
whatever their skin

Big Business

'all we know is
that the men we all work with
are the same as us…'

0161 2036313
www.cashgenerator.co.uk
CASH GENERATOR
The Buy, Sell
& Loan Store
INSTANT CHEQUE CASHING
Lowest rates guaranteed
INSTANT CHEQUE CASHING
Lowest rates guaranteed
WESTERN UNION

132 more

the new boss from the company behind the takeover
came in to give us all a pep talk
to ease the uncertainty and fears we all had
of maybe losing our jobs
and to paint for us all a vision of the future

in groups of 10
we were all given a time slot
when we had to be in the boardroom
to listen to this man

this man who had never made a delivery to anyone anywhere
this man who whenever he got a parking ticket or CCTV fine
had only to make sure that it was entered correctly onto his expense account
this man who had never had to also hold down a weekend job
hauling 25lb boxes of frozen lamb into the backs of trucks
for £6.50 an hour after tax
just so he could afford to take his kids to the cinema

this man who had the charm and charisma of a politician
rather than the blunt edges of a worker
this man who smiled at us and looked at us straight in the eye
and told us that we were important
what he liked to call "the oxygen of this company"
which his shareholders had bought
and how it just wouldn't make any sense
to get rid of any one of us
would it?

this man who 6 months later
made the decision on behalf of his shareholders
to shut down our workshop
laying off 7 mechanics
so that all of the repairs and maintenance of our vehicles
could be done by the new company's already existing network
of garages and service centres

this man who lives away in the country
off with the fairies

who is placed under so much pressure
every minute of the day by his shareholders
to increase the bottom line
slowly stripping away all of his humanity and heart
so that with one swoosh of his pen
he can turn upside down 7 people's lives
and still sleep at night
and still play frisbee with his kids on a beach
knowing that he has lied
to 132 more

all we know is

we will never know what is inside the brain of the CEO
who owns this company we all work for
we will never know from where or why
he makes these decisions about our bonuses getting stopped
or why our overtime rate
is so derisory

we will never know what it is like
to twist a pair of rugby ball cufflinks
so that they are positioned perfectly straight
on the ends of a £200 shirt
or what smoking a £50 cigar feels like

we will never know what it is like
to put our foot down on an accelerator pedal
that shoots a Bentley off down the road
at close to what feels like security
or how it feels
making a decision
that will squeeze a man in a fist until he pops
or how it feels
firing off an email to HR
telling them that 7 human beings will not be needed anymore
and need to be processed off the premises
as cheaply as possible

all we do know
is that the men we all work with
are the same as us
that they have to pay the same bills as us
because if they don't
then their roof will be taken away
and then the love of their woman will be taken away
all we know is that we continually worry
about keeping our jobs
just like you do
because if we didn't have them

then there wouldn't be any food on the table
or shoes for the children's feet
or an internet connection
or laughter and wine

all we know is
that the CEO who owns this company we all work for
is not worried about what we know anymore
because he has reached such a lofty level
that he can't even hear us
and even if he pulled the hearts out of half of his staff's chests
or immolated the twenty best workers of the 400 he employs
then it would affect him and his family
by less than 0.1%

and that, unfortunately
isn't readily taught in the schools
but only learnt
or told
in poems and songs
like this one

dragging our knuckles across the bone-littered floor

if we can plant our feet on the surface of the moon
and see into the back rooms of the universe
only using a piece of glass
if we can put our eyes inside the tip of a cable
so that they can be taken down
into the depths of the ocean
if we can slip
slivers of metal into the side of a phone
that turns them into circuses
into market squares
then why can't we muster the will
to create systems in which everybody
has a job that pays them enough money
to put water and food
into the mouths of their families?

if we can split something invisible to the naked eye
and release what's left
so that it can power whole cities with electricity and heat
light and communication
then why can't we erect roofs
to go over every head in those same
cities too?

if we can spend thousands of pounds
to travel halfway around the globe
just to save a single chimpanzee
if we can all pull together
to save minke whales
stranded on a beach

if we can bring back to life
almost dead species
using just the fierce love
that we carry around inside us
then why can't we show
the same humility and grace
to the woman sat on the corner of Edgware Road

who has spent so many hours exposed to the cold
that she has completely shut down
and fallen asleep
with her chin on her chest
and her hands held out?

if we can excavate a piece of rock from the Antarctic
and peer into it
using lasers and spectrometers
only to be able to predict the exact age of the Universe
to within one single century
if we can
predict
where all of the stars and planets in this Universe will be
at any stage over the next 4 billion years
to within 0.01% of accuracy
then why were we unable to predict
that when it came to each other
we would remain cavemen
dragging our knuckles across the bone-littered floor?

our guts and our hands

he invited me back to his houseboat for drinks some weekends
and we'd sit there
on the top of it
smoking and drinking wine
and I'd listen to this man who was dying of cancer who had spent
50 years in the system of work
who had the letters S-C-A-V-E-N-G-E
tattooed across the fingers of his hands
telling me about how we should
never give up raging
never give up fighting
until the day we die
because that was exactly what they wanted us to do
because they know that they can never be beaten
telling me it was an imperative
that we keep on standing up
after getting knocked down
raging
rattling the bars of our cages
because raging was our only hope
as he turned up The Who on his portable stereo
telling me to be careful
because a man in a rage should choose his battles carefully
and never let his heart get strung out
fighting on too many fronts
because they'll end up eating him up
and make him feel like it is all his own fault
that he feels like he is going insane

then after she'd put the kids to bed
his girlfriend came up to join us
and we'd all sit together on the top of his boat
smoking and drinking wine
laughing together
realising at about 2 am
that our guts and our hands
were the only things we had left
to hold on to

this job is all we have to protect us

there is only this job between us
and the man stood on the corner of Edgware Rd and Praed Street
outside the Metropole Hotel
holding his hands out to passersby
who are heading towards their jobs

there is only this job between us
and the lady sat on the corner of Edgware and Marylebone Rd
crouched between the phone box and M&S
unable to hold out her polystyrene cup anymore
because she's gotten so tired from the night spent exposed to the cold
that she's fallen asleep
with her chin on her chest

there is only this job between us
and the man who goes along Edgware Rd every morning at 6 am
scurrying through the bins to see if he can find any food to eat
or any cigarette butts with half an inch left on them
to smoke

there is only this job between us
and the man who knows that it is just a matter of time now
before the eviction notice comes through the door
before the bailiffs come banging
starting that slide into becoming one of those men and women
dotted along Edgware Rd

there is only this job
that keep our women in love with us
and our children sat on our laps
these jobs
that keep us inches away from insanity
which give us beds and wine to soften us up every night
just so we can go out and do it all over again
tomorrow

and they wonder
why when they threaten to take them away
we get so agitated
and angry

you can't work at a control point for 11 hours a day

you can't work at a control point for 11 hours a day and not ask why
so much importance is placed on the delivery of a document
when a woman in the room next door
has to visit a food bank every other night
to beg for a bag of pasta
because her 40 hour a week telephonist job
doesn't provide her with enough money
to feed her children

you can't work at a control point for 11 hours a day and not learn sympathy
for the man with only one leg
who every day sits propped up against the phone box on Edgware Road
holding his hands out for change
as you pass him by on the way to your job

you can't work at a control point for 11 hours a day and not learn humility
for the couriers who have to sit on their bikes
and drive around London
only to earn the same money as us controllers earn
in half the time it takes them to do that job

you can't work at a control point for 11 hours a day and not go home to a flat at night
with wine, heat and hot water
and not wonder
that despite all the probes we have sent into space
and all the hands and feet we have put on the moon
and all the rivers and seas we have held back
and all the almost dead species we have saved
why we still haven't yet managed
to produce a system
in which every man woman and child
has access
to a roof over their heads

you can't work at a control point for 11 hours a day
and not learn to see the world like this
or if you can
then you are most probably not a controller anymore
but a supervisor

no perspective

as we sit in our controllers' chairs
fretting about picking up cakes and drums of ink
fashion garments and printed documents
being pressured by our supervisors
to get them all delivered on time,
other people wonder where their next litre of water will come from
or if they will ever get the chance
to eat a piece of meat again

as we fume and steam that we have been put on the late shift
for the third consecutive week running
and take our fuming and steaming to the HR manager
demanding to know if there is some kind of plot underway
to "manage us out of the business",
23 year old commanders
decide to machete to death whole families
just because they are from a different tribe

as we sit in our comfortable controllers' chairs
drinking coffee and tapping away at our keypads
moaning about the way our women try to dictate our lives
and how if it carries on
then we are going to have to consider
leaving that "moany fucking bitch"
along with those two kids we fathered,
4 year olds get washed up on an Italian beach
because their families were trying to get to a land
where the woman wouldn't get raped
and the man put in a cell for over 20 years
just for stealing a kilo of flour

as we bemoan the hours we put in doing this job
placed under what we consider intolerable pressures
trying to balance the needs of the clients and couriers
having our jobs threatened each day
by supervisors we consider to be on the same rung as dictators
unable to cover the bills and debt payments each month
thinking all the time that we are not paid
anywhere near enough for what we do,

others sit in makeshift camps
or roam the streets with nowhere to go
happy at least that they are not now in their land
where their dictators chopped off the hands of a man
just for stroking the cheek of his wife
in a public square

when we come home completely stressed
from the 11 hour shifts we've put in
drinking wine, bitching
about how the supervisor only picked us up on the 4 or 5 jobs we fucked up
without taking into consideration the hundreds of others
that we made happen
falling asleep in our comfortable beds
to dream of holidays and sex
others have trouble falling asleep at all
and dream that if only they could have the same problems
as those controllers
then they wouldn't have to cower under their beds
every time they heard a helicopter
approaching overhead

controllers
in their £400 a-week-take-home controlling jobs
have always had problems
getting things into perspective

as the poets write about the smell of their dead fathers' tweed jackets

a crust of dry bread has become the dream of millions
running water and one bar of electric heat
amenities out of reach for a quarter of the globe
as CEOs stand in their kitchens
warming their feet on underground heated slate tiles
while peeling an avocado slate
ripped from the earth by people whose hands have to squeeze the last drop of milk
from a dead breast
wring a sleeping bag dry
so they can sleep at night without freezing their guts
people who have jobs but still have to queue in foodbanks just to feed their families
as their Prime Ministers and Presidents talk about nuclear wars
destroy
whole communities with an idea they had while playing a round of golf
people who once worked on a farm or in a call centre or under the ground
who now have no jobs because of an agreement signed on a jet
30,000 feet above the clouds
people who are moved on from country to country
unwanted
who have to live in makeshift camps for years
just because their God lost an election
and had His fingertips replaced on the trigger of a gun
people who can't clothe or take their children on a holiday anymore
because the price of oil drained from the ground 5000 miles away shot up into the
sky
and closed all of their factories
people who once worked in industries long ago shut by progress
who once used their hands to rivet together ships haul a piece of steel out of a blast
furnace replace
the heart of a 12 year old girl hand over a cup of tea to a miner squeeze
tomato ketchup into a factory worker's bacon sandwich
who now sit at home with nothing to do

using those same hands to put together 1000 piece jigsaw puzzles
or knit hats for their grandchildren who will grow up to be a number
on a list of numbers who don't have any jobs

as the poets write about the smell of their dead fathers' tweed jackets
are Forwarded £5,000 for a poem about the opening of a wardrobe
have enough time on their hands
to stand in front of mirrors
contemplating whether they exist or not
and books about wizards and bondage
sell millions

Rise

'...makes them want to rise,
burst out of hands,
head towards the sun....'

ALTAIF MONEY
TRANSFER

Rise

the job grinds people down
until they feel like bits of dust,
the job they have to keep hold of
like a dying sparrow in their hands
grinds people down

all of the hours spent dipping their shoulder
and charging at the sun
carrying this dying little sparrow
in their hands
has made them feel bone-tired,
they are exhausted
and close to giving up

the dying little sparrow has almost killed them,
the bills the CCJ's
the rent arrears utility bills dentist's bills internet payments
food roof beer shoes shirts, all of it,
has almost killed the very centre of them

the fear of losing everything
has made them supple enough
to accept almost anything

but only almost
because the holding of hands with a woman under a blood-red sun
and the wine that drips down from rib to rib
to form puddles in the gut
and the music
that lifts sparrows up
back onto their feet,
makes them want to rise,
burst out of hands,
head towards the sun, sit
on wires tin roofs chimney pipes
to sing sing sing
about that unconquerable little bit of them,
how that will never die
like a little sparrow in a pair of hands
however tightly they squeeze it

when a saxophone or a pen were the only weapons we needed

I remember the days before we were owned by big corporations
when controllers used to come into work hungover from the night before
after they had drunk wine until they couldn't stand up
or put their arms around their woman
and whisper into her ear that they still loved her those days

when they still knew that they would keep their jobs and get another chance
to make things right I remember
the days when controllers used to be allowed to take random breaks
and go outside to smoke a cigarette looking up at the sky
while talking to their colleagues about politics and Prime Ministers
thinking that there still was a chance to save the homeless man
sat on the corner of Edgware Rd holding his hands out for change
as they passed him by on the way to work
to save
the alcoholic woman in the flat next door
who kept them awake all night playing Nina Simone on her stereo at full blast

when they still thought
that they could save the NHS and the press and the education system
when they could
still lay out on a Saturday afternoon after 5 days of 11 hour shifts
sipping at a cold beer on grass greener than emeralds under trees
that talked to each other in the wind
waiting for the stars to shine in the night sky like bonfires of hope without
insecurity and fear crawling all over their bodies like ants I remember
those days when we didn't have to take random breathalyser tests
before we started our 11 hour shifts
and the supervisor sending us home if we failed when there wasn't
a Tesco Express on every street and communities would gather
outside corner shops to talk about their daughters and sons
who were leaving home and starting their first job
in the bright enchanted world I remember
the days before everything became a commodity
before jobs became mere numbers that could be fed into a machine
only to not come out the other side where land
once propped up youth clubs in which teenagers
could get excited about their first kiss

where land held up libraries where men and women could get away from the cold
and come across the words of Blake or Bukowski our land
that has now been sold off to entrepreneurs and corporations

where blocks of luxury flats glisten in the sun stars
hang in the night sky over
too far away now
for any of their hope to reach us

when footballers didn't earn more in a second
than controllers nurses firemen teachers call centre operators and factory workers
earn in a week

where a pub landlord would welcome in a group of men
rather than telling their staff to keep an eye on them where
you could walk anywhere even into the sun
and pull out a saxophone or a pen
only to sing
that everyone still had a chance
and people would actually believe it

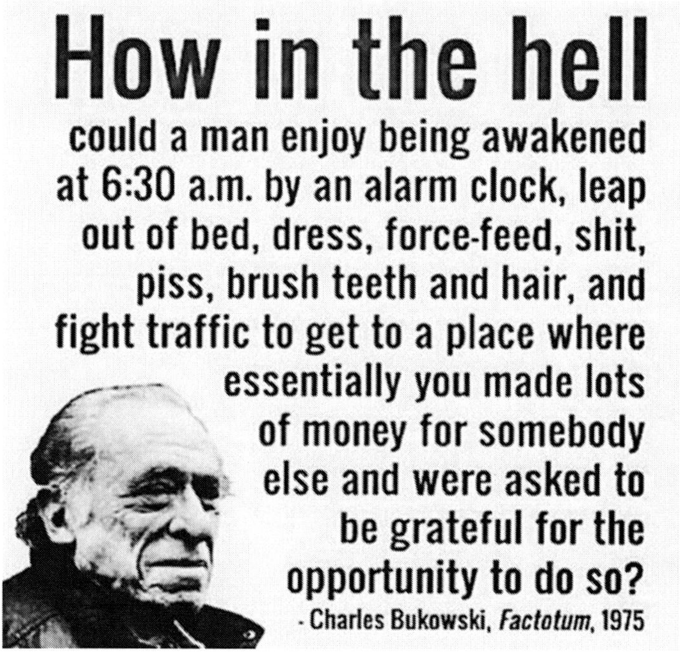

stitching this universe together

Sadiq wants to stay a part of this control room, a part
of this bunch of chained cynical indebted men
who continually take the piss out of his haircuts
his shoes and his love life
who never cut him any slack whenever he makes a mistake
laughing and calling him names that Sadiq laughs back at
because Sadiq knows
that he will be a part of that pack in a couple of hours
and that the hands he uses to twist the shoes onto his 2 year old's feet every morning
and that wrap the scarf around her neck to keep her warm
and that slip her coat over her shoulders by the door
are the same hands as Mikey's and Bill's and Dermot's and Javed's
who every morning slip and wrap the same shoes and scarves and coats
around their children

Antoine wants to stay a part of this control room, even when it is him
who is on the receiving end of his fellow controller's cruelty
taking the mickey out of him getting bollocked by one of the supervisors
as they circle and sharpen their minds
waiting for the quietest moment possible
before launching their one liners and cusses
into his ears
causing the rest of the pack to crack up in fits of laughter
because Antoine knows that all of this
is done in the name of survival
a survival that enables Antoine to put cereal on the table in front of his 6 year old boy pour
milk into his wife's coffee cup keep
the car topped up with diesel the lights burning the roof solid the water hot the sun up in the sky
warming all of our hands and backs as we punch buttons on keypads lift
quarter ton engines out of vans haul
filing cabinets from one office into another office
and all because
we need to protect those castles
that we can safely pack our lives away in
whenever it gets cold

Stacey wants to stay a part of this control room
where despite all of the bollockings and bloodlettings she has been on the end of
she keeps getting up after being knocked down
constantly talking with enthusiasm about her end games, her outs
which this control room is going to give to her
which has her sitting on beaches lying next to Calvin Klein models
balancing Campari and sodas on their ripped stomachs
or behind the steering wheel of a 35 grand sports car
heading into a sunset the colour of a burning boys heart

or sat on the edge of a pool
dangling her feet in the water behind her paid-for home
with the sun holding her hand
and the ocean salting her hair
the same dreams in fact
that the woman sitting next to you on the bus has
that the woman typing figures into a computer terminal all day has
that the woman who scans your shopping at the checkout has
that the man sat at the top of a crane or in the cabin of a van has
the same dreams of freedom
that we all have
where we won't anymore have to put up with a man
who feels the need to dehumanise and bully us in front of a room full of people
just because he is paid 4 times more
and has a reputation to keep

we all want to stay a part of this control room
for as long as possible
or at least until our hands cannot tap one single button more
on one of their keypads
or at least until our minds have given up
and can't see through the hundreds of jobs
that keep dropping down onto our screens
or at least until our blood
stops foaming with this adrenalin
which allows us to understand and get through
all of those busy Friday afternoons
because in the end
don't we need these jobs
for more than just their money
don't we need these jobs

so that we can stand in front of mirrors
and look at ourselves
without feeling worthless
or disconnected
like a CEO must
like a President or Prime Minister must
like the head of an HR department must
don't we need these jobs
in the same way that Martin Luther King needed his dream
in the same way that Rosa Parks needed to stay on that bus
in the same way that the Wilding needed equality
that gravity
pulls on the planets and stars
the same way that the sea
can never stop being the sea

we all want to stay a part of this control room
for as long as possible
because this is where we learnt
that the men and women who are employed by Phoenix Express
are the same
as every working man
and woman
and that all of our fingertips combined
might just be the fingertips
that keep us and this Universe
stitched together

UNDERGROUN
EDGWARE ROAD STATION
Bakerloo line
Aldwych

the blood and smiles yet to be delivered into this world

we move the beds of shut down hospital wards that our grandparents laid in to die
we carry the blood of children still open on operating tables
from blood banks to theatres
just to see if they will live
we pack transit vans full of cakes
and take them to weddings where daughters will be given away to men
we pick up contracts from big lawyers and deliver them to CEOs who work from home
so that they can proofread them and sign off the building of a dam
that will shut down a river and turn villages into dust
we tap away at keypads all day sending instructions to couriers
to drive their big vans to bankrupt companies
so that they can empty them of the desks and chairs that workers once sat in
earning just enough money to feed their families and pay their rent
we pick up artificial limbs from factories and deliver them to hospitals
so that men who lost a leg in a war 5,000 miles away
can learn to walk again
we place couriers outside big banks at 2 am
in case the money markets in countries far away take a dive or soar into the sky
we pick up hearts at road traffic accidents
and rush them off to clinics
so that they can be frozen before they stop beating
we put barrels of ink into the backs of vans
and deliver them to printers in Truro and Dunfermline
so that they can print eviction notices and final demand notices we move
dead people's bodies
after they have been stripped of their organs
and sewed back up as a mark of respect we pick up
projectors screens whiteboards brochures lecterns
and deliver them to conference rooms in hotels
so that a man from one of the big banks can stand in front of 200 people
and explain to them why more and more acquisitions and the swallowing up of jobs
is the best way to grow and thread a corporation through with steel and strength

and when our shifts have finished
we go home to play with our daughters and sons picking up plastic tea pots
pouring imaginary tea into plastic cups while sat at imaginary tea parties we make
big engine noises come out of our throats as we help them steer their toy trucks
to the piles of wooden blocks

that they load onto those trucks and steer back across to the other side of the room
where they unload them and announce to their world that "everything has been delivered"
where we pick up bottles of wine after they have gone to bed
and sit at a window wondering about the industries of men
and the blood and smiles that are still yet to be delivered into this world
whether or not they will be the ones
to write that song or poem   start
the revolution
that will change everything